FOOD & FEASTS

in

Ancient Greece

Imogen Dawson

new
Discovery
B·O·O·K·S
Parsippany, New Jersey

First American publication 1995 by New Discovery Books,
an imprint of Silver Burdett Press.
A Simon & Schuster Company
299 Jefferson Road, Parsippany, NJ 07054

First published in 1995 in Great Britain by
Wayland (Publishers) Ltd

A ZOË BOOK

Devised and produced by
Zoë Books Limited
15 Worthy Lane
Winchester
Hampshire SO23 7AB
England

Printed in Italy by Grafedit SpA.
Design: Jan Sterling, Sterling Associates
Picture research: Victoria Sturgess
Maps: Gecko Limited
Production: Grahame Griffiths

10 9 8 7 6 5 4 3 2 1

Library of Congress Cataloging-in-Publication Data

Dawson, Imogen.
    Food & feasts in ancient Greece / Imogen Dawson.
        p.cm. — (Food & feasts)
    Includes bibliographical references and index.
    ISBN 0-02-726329-0
    1. Diet—Greece—Juvenile literature. 2. Cookery,
Greek—Juvenile literature. 3. Food habits—Greece—
Juvenile literature. [1. Food habits—Greece. 2. Cookery,
Greek. 3. Greece—Social life and customs.] I. Title. II.
Title: Food and feasts in ancient Greece. III. Series.
TX360.G85D39 1995
394.1'0938—dc20   94-32495

Summary: A social history of the ancient Greeks in Europe,
explaining what foods were eaten and describing how
they were prepared or cooked. Includes information about
events that brought about special celebrations and feasts.

Photographic acknowledgments

The publishers wish to acknowledge, with thanks, the
following photographic sources:

Acropolis Museum, Athens 18b, 24t; DDA Photo Library
title page, 4t, 7t, 9t, 11t, 12t, 13t, 15t&b, 18t, 19t&b, 21b;
C. M. Dixon 3, 4b, 6t&b, 7b, 8t&b, 9b, 10t&b, 11b,
12bl&br, 13b, 14b, 16b, 20t&b, 21t, 22b, 24b, 25; Lesley
& Roy Adkins Picture Library 17b; Louvre, Paris 22t;
Mandralisca Museum, Sicily 16t; Metropolitan Museum
of Art, New York 23t; National Museum, Athens 5t, 17t;
Staatliche Museen, Berlin 14t.

Cover: C. M. Dixon top left, center, top right, bottom
right; Louvre, Paris bottom left.

The publishers have made every effort to trace the
copyright holders, but if they have inadvertently
overlooked any, they will be pleased to make the
necessary arrangement at the first opportunity.

Contents

Introduction

Some areas of mainland Greece are cut off from each other by mountains. The people who settled in these areas had little contact with one another and had different ways of life.

▽ This pottery figure shows a woman cooking over an open fire. The large pots for preparing soups and stews were often made of clay. Sometimes iron pots, or **cauldrons**, were used instead.

The weather in Greece is warm and mild for most of the year. More than 3,000 years ago, people in ancient Greece spent much of their time outdoors. Most food was prepared and then cooked outside on an open fire. Fruit, vegetables, and **herbs** were often dried outside in the sun to **preserve** them.

Many people lived and worked near the sea, where there was good farmland. The farmers could not grow enough food crops for everyone, so supplies of grain and other foods such as pepper and spices were brought in, or **imported**, from other lands.

The farmers planted olive trees and grapevines. The olive oil and wine they made could be sold to many different places in Europe and the Middle East. Most goods were transported by sea, because sea travel was easier than land travel. The ancient Greeks were skilled at shipbuilding, sailing, and fishing.

△ Olive trees cover the mountainsides and the valley below the remains of the ancient buildings at Delphi.

Olive oil was used not only for cooking but also as fuel for lamps and in making soaps and perfumes.

△ Olive oil and wine were stored and transported in large pottery jars called **amphorae**.

This beautifully decorated amphora was made for a funeral display and was not for everyday use.

The rise and fall of the ancient Greeks

2,500 – 1,000 B.C.: Greek-speaking peoples settle in Greece. Mycenae becomes a powerful center.

800 – 500 B.C. Athens and other cities grow in importance. Greek settlements arise in Italy, France, and North Africa.

500 – 338 B.C.: The Persians attack the Greeks and are defeated. Wars take place between Greek cities, particularly Athens and Sparta.

338 – 31 B.C.: The Greeks lose their independence. Philip of Macedon invades Greece. His son, Alexander the Great, defeats the Persians. He founds many Greek cities in the lands he rules, which stretch from Egypt to India.

After Alexander's death in 323 B.C., many Greeks settle in Egypt and Syria. The Romans become more powerful. Many Greek settlements in Europe are ruled from Rome. Finally, after a battle in 31 B.C., Greece itself is ruled by the Romans.

The ancient Greeks used spices such as nutmeg, cinnamon, and cloves in their food. These spices were imported from Egypt and the Middle East.

The ancient Greeks kept slaves to do much of the work in rich households and on large farms. Some slaves could buy their freedom or were freed by their owners.

In Ancient Greece, people usually ate more fish and seafood than meat. Sometimes oxen, sheep, and **game**, such as wild boar, were roasted on a **spit** over the fire, for a feast.

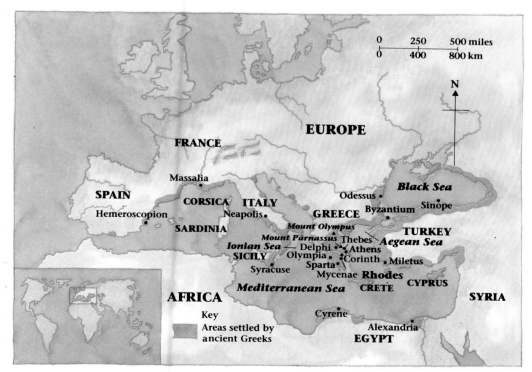

◁ This map shows where the ancient Greeks lived and settled over a period of 1,500 years, until they were ruled by the Romans.

▽ A clay tablet from Pylos with Mycenaean writing

▽ This wall painting is from Tiryns. It was made by people from Mycenae, in the 12th or 13th century B.C., and shows a hunt for wild boar.

Poorer people rarely ate fish or meat. They made soups and stews from vegetables such as peas and beans. They ate *maza*—flatbread or cakes made from grain paste—with olives, cheese, and eggs. There was plenty of fresh or dried fruit such as figs and grapes to eat. Sometimes people drank wine, which they mixed with water to make it weaker, but usually they drank milk or water with their meals.

People who lived in towns bought fresh food from the open air market, the agora. The men did the shopping while the women stayed at home to work and run the household. The men went to the agora every morning to shop and to meet their friends.

In the evenings some households held parties called symposia, when the men and their guests ate, drank, and talked until the early hours of the morning.

Cities such as Athens and Sparta controlled large areas of the countryside around them. They were **city-states**. In times of war, farmers and fishermen became soldiers and sailors, fighting to defend their city-state.

Each city-state made its own laws and was ruled in different ways. Sparta was ruled by powerful families. Farmworkers, called helots, could not leave the land and were treated like slaves.

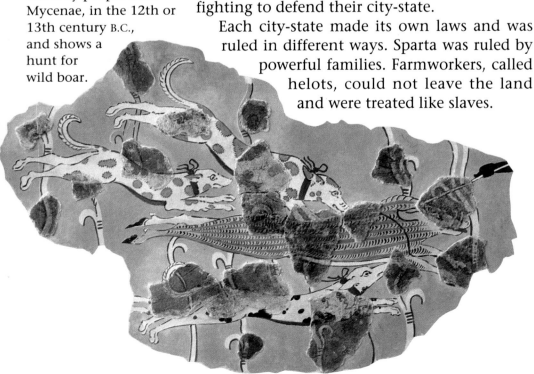

Hippocrates was a doctor and writer who lived in the 5th century B.C. He wrote one of the most important books about medicine. His ideas about health are still important today.

The ancient Greeks knew that keeping clean and fit, eating fresh food, and drinking clean water would help to keep them healthy.

The ancient Greeks wrote many books about food and cooking. Achestratus, who lived in the 4th century B.C., was one of the most important cooking writers. He was said to have "traveled the lands and seas in his desire to test the delights of the stomach."

from *The Gastronomers*, by Athenaeus, written in the 2nd century A.D.

△ The Parthenon was built by the Athenians to celebrate their victory over the Persians. It took nine years to build and was completed in 432 B.C. Archaeologists are still at work on this site in the middle of Athens.

The rulers of Athens were freely chosen, or **elected**, by the people who were born there. In 508 B.C. Athens became the first **democracy**.

The ancient Greeks were great thinkers and writers. Many of their works—in literature (plays and poetry) and in mathematics, science, and medicine—have survived, which is why we know so much about the Greeks.

There are also remains of buildings and **artifacts**, such as pottery, jewelry, and sculptures, in many of the places where the ancient Greeks settled. **Archaeologists** dig up, or **excavate**, these sites. They examine these remains very carefully.

▽ The ancient Greeks lay down to eat at **banquets**, as shown in this bronze figure, made around 530 B.C.

In Sparta people lay on hard wooden benches, but in other places they lay on *kline*. These were couches covered with folded cloth to make them softer. *Kline* were also used as beds.

Farming and food in the countryside

The winters in the mountains of mainland Greece can be cold and wet, but the summers are warm and dry. Near the coast and on most of the islands the climate is milder. The winters are warmer and the summers are hot.

In the time of the ancient Greeks, many of the hills and mountains were covered by woodland and forests. People gathered the almonds, figs, walnuts, grapes, and olives that grew wild. They hunted for animals and birds that lived in the woods and forests. They ate game such as hare, deer, partridge, and wild boar. People used bows and arrows or spears for hunting. They kept hunting dogs to help them to find the game and to bring back the birds that were killed. They also set traps to catch some of the smaller animals.

Trees were cut down and the wood was used as fuel in household fireplaces. Small areas of land were cleared to grow crops, such as grain and beans. The soil was not rich enough for crops to grow well, but the people could grow enough food to survive.

People kept herds of sheep and goats. These animals could survive in cold weather and would search, or **forage**, for food on the hills and mountainsides. Most of the milk the sheep and goats produced was used to make

△ This scene of a hunter and his dog bringing back hares is painted on a drinking cup called a kylix. It was made in about 550 B.C.

"A working woman, rising before dawn to spin and needing light . . . piles brushwood on a smoldering log, and the whole heap . . . goes up in a mighty blaze."

from *The Voyage of Argo*, by Apollonius of Rhodes, written in the 3rd century B.C.

People kept bees for honey, which was used as a sweetener in food. Sugar was unknown in ancient Greece.

▽ A clay figure of a woman kneeling in front of the fire. She fans the fire to bring air to it. Then the fire will burst into flame.

△ Small patches of snow still lie on the higher slopes of Mount Parnassus, even in early June when the yellow broom flowers.

everyday foods such as yogurt and cheeses. The rest of the milk was drunk or added to foods such as porridge.

Poorer people rarely killed these animals for meat, except for a feast. Then they spit-roasted young animals whole over an open fire. Larger animals were cut up. Some parts of the animals were roasted and other parts were added to vegetable soups or stews. These were often cooked in earthenware pots, which were held in position over the fire by iron **trivets**.

People used the animal skins to make shoes and clothes such as capes, which they wore during the day and wrapped round them during the winter nights. Skins were also used to make containers for carrying water and other drinks.

▽ In this stone carving, a shepherd carries a ram over his shoulders.

"I love to sit on a rock in the shade with wine to drink, a cake of cheese, goat's milk and some meat—from a young cow or a kid."

from *Works and Days*, by Hesiod

▽ This clay figure is of a man who is about to cut up a pig.

△ Meat and vegetables are being cooked on skewers, over an open-air fire.

The Spartans' black broth, said to have been made from pork stock, salt, and vinegar, was famous all over ancient Greece.

"Early in the morning, at dawn, we would put some plump small birds on the fire, then the roasted flesh of a pig . . . then we would wash them down with sweet wine."

from *The Sirens*, by Epicharmus, written about 400 B.C.

In some woodland areas of Greece, people kept pigs to slaughter for meat. These animals were fed on food scraps and also foraged for acorns, beechnuts, and other food in the woods.

Meat from pigs was prepared and cooked in many different ways. Small pieces of pork were added to soups and stews or put on sticks, or **skewers**, with vegetables such as onions. The skewered meat was cooked over the fire. Meat from the pig could also be chopped or ground and made into sausages or meatballs.

Larger pieces of meat were roasted over the fire. In winter some of this meat was preserved. Sometimes whole legs, or **hams**, were rubbed with salt and then hung high over the fire to dry in the smoke. Pieces of pork were also salted and then put in pots with herbs and pickled in wine vinegar.

Only a few parts of Greece had enough rainfall and good soil for grass to grow well enough to feed cattle. One area was Boeotia (which means cowland), where the farmer and writer Hesiod lived.

Other fruits, such as apples and pears, and vegetables such as celery, leeks, and garlic also grew wild in parts of Greece. At first, people simply gathered these for

△ A woman sits in the shade of a fruit tree, and a bowl of food is brought to her.

food. Later they **cultivated** these plants and trees and grew fruit and vegetables as crops.

Farmers planted trees and grapevines on strips of land, or **terraces**, on the hillsides. The terraces helped to keep the soil moist, as water drained away more slowly. They also helped to prevent storms from washing away the soil.

There were many freshwater springs and streams that provided good clean drinking water, particularly in the hills and mountains. Because there was little rain during the summer months, there was often a **drought**. Sometimes farmers used water from rivers and springs to water, or **irrigate**, their crops.

"There are two springs. One feeds little streams of water to all parts of the field. The other is used by the people as a watering place."

from Homer's *Odyssey*. This long poem was probably composed in the 8th century B.C.

▽ The large jug on the left was used to serve water. The small jug at the back was for wine. The jug at the front, with a small neck, was used to serve olive oil.

"... the sweet apple turning red at the top of the highest branch, forgotten by the apple-gatherers—no, not quite forgotten, for they could not reach so far ..."

from a fragment of a poem by Sappho. She lived on the island of Lesbos, in the 6th century B.C.

△ Zeus drinks from a cup made from an ox horn.

The ancient Greeks believed in a family of gods and goddesses, whose home was on Mount Olympus, the highest mountain in Greece. The father of the gods was Zeus, who protected Greece. Zeus controlled the skies and sent the rain, wind, and thunderstorms. Poseidon, his brother, ruled the rivers and seas. He could cause earthquakes and storms. Hestia, the older sister of Zeus, was goddess of the household fire. She protected the home and the family. She was the goddess most loved by the ancient Greeks.

▽ This painting on a bowl was made in the 5th century B.C. It shows Apollo, the god of light, music, and healing, pouring wine on the ground as an offering, probably to his father, Zeus.

The gods and goddesses played a large part in the everyday life of the ancient Greeks. Whenever they drank water or wine, the Greeks poured a little of it on the ground, as a gift for the gods.

Farmers asked the gods to protect their families, animals, and crops. Sometimes they would prepare a feast and offer some of the food to the gods. Often this food was left on a simple table, or **altar**, in the fields.

"Make prayers to Zeus the farmer's god and to Demeter, for her grain, to make it ripe and heavy."

from *Works and Days*, by Hesiod

At first the ancient Greeks were **subsistence** farmers. They kept a few animals and grew enough food for their families to eat. If their crops failed, there was a **famine** and people died of hunger.

Grain was the most important, or **staple**, crop. Wheat was grown in the few areas where the soil was good. Barley was grown in many places. The seeds were soaked in water and then cooked as porridge or soup. Barley seeds were also used to make *maza*, from grain

▽ A hand mill, or **quern**, was used for grinding seeds such as wheat or barley.

▷ Demeter, the sister of Zeus, was the goddess of the fruits of the earth. The ancient Greeks believed that she taught the farmers how to grow corn. Here she is shown on the left holding corn. Persephone, her daughter, is on the right.

Bread or grain paste was often the only cooked food people ate each day: "For a long time they let their hand mills stand idle and lived on uncooked food."

from *The Voyage of Argo*, by Apollonius of Rhodes

▽ These clay figures show women preparing to bake bread. The dome-shaped oven is in the background.

Sometimes the dough was divided into eight slices before the loaf was cooked. Then it could be easily separated into portions when the bread was ready to eat.

paste. The seeds were ground in a hand mill and then mixed with oil and spices, such as coriander, and shaped into flat cakes.

Only rich people could afford to make or buy loaves of bread made from wheat rather than barley. The dough was placed on an earthenware pan and a heated domed lid, or an upturned pot, was put over the top to make an individual oven for the loaf. Embers from the fire were heaped over the lid, so that the bread baked in the heat underneath it.

△ This painting on a cup was made around the 6th century B.C. It shows a man plowing with two oxen.

Farmers used oxen to pull their wooden plows and carts. Mules were often used to pull heavy loads in the hills and mountains. Most farmers rode donkeys rather than horses.

More and more trees were cut down because the wood was needed to build houses, farm carts and tools, and especially ships.

Wood was also needed to make **charcoal**. Metalworkers used charcoal to make their fires as hot as possible. Then they could bend and shape the metals they worked with more easily. They used iron to make many different tools and weapons.

As the forests were cut down, game birds and animals became rare. Without the trees there was not enough food and shelter for the wildlife.

The soil on the hillsides and mountains became poorer. The trees had protected the soil from being washed away and **eroded** by heavy

"Some of the mountains now provide food only for bees. Not so long ago there were timber roofs, cut from the trees growing there, which were large enough to cover the biggest houses."

from *Critias*, by Plato, written in the 4th century B.C.

"Mules use their great strength to drag some beam or huge timber down the mountain along a rugged track."

from *The Iliad*, by Homer, probably composed in the 8th century B.C.

◁ Goats can survive even where there is little to eat. However, they eat young shoots and prevent grass, bushes, and trees from growing well.

Olive trees do not produce a good crop of olives until they are about 14 years old.

The Spartans, who were at war with the Athenians, invaded Attica and cut down the olive trees.

rain and wind. Few crops could be grown on the soil that remained.

As the city-states became stronger and trade grew with other lands, more people lived in the towns and cities. Farmers began to sell their extra, or **surplus**, food to the townspeople. They took fresh fruit, vegetables, and herbs to the marketplaces every day.

Olives and grapes became the most important crops for the farmers, as more and more olive oil and wine were **exported**. Olive trees were planted all over the country. They took much of the remaining nourishment out of the soil. Then there was not enough good soil to grow the grain crops to feed all the people.

In some areas, particularly in Attica, within the city-state of Athens, farmers grew mostly vines and olives. They kept only a small number of farm animals. Meat became scarce.

Some farmers became rich. They sold grapes and olives for cash and bought grain, salt, and spices as well as the other goods they needed for their families and farms. However, many farmers could not survive. They left the land to live in the towns or went to farm in Greek settlements abroad.

△ The ancient Greeks used wood to make furniture for their houses. This vase painting shows a woman sitting on a chair while her hair is being done. The wooden chest the slave is carrying was used to store clothes.

▷ Olive trees and vines grow in Attica today.

Food from the sea

▷ The customer waits while a fresh tuna fish is cut up for him.

▽ A Mycenaean storage jar decorated with a painting of an octopus. The octopus flesh would be beaten against the rocks before it was cooked, to make it tender enough to eat.

Fish was often served with sour grapes. The juice was sharp, like lemons served with fish today. Lemons were unknown in ancient Greece.

Many people in ancient Greece lived close to the sea. Fishing boats could sail for most of the year, except during the winter storms. Some people caught fish and seafood from the shores or gathered shellfish from the rocks. There was a good supply of fish and seafood for most of the year.

People usually ate fresh fish and seafood, but fish was also preserved to be eaten in the winter months. Fish such as cod were salted and dried in the sun.

If the fishermen did not sell all their fresh fish, they sometimes pickled it. They used oil and vinegar, and herbs such as dill or fennel, which grew wild. Pickled mackerel or sardines are called *savoro*.

At first, when meat was more plentiful, fish was eaten mainly by poorer people.

"He dives with ease, he leaps from the sails and gathers oysters for twenty men."

from *The Iliad*, by Homer

Later, when meat became scarce, fish such as red mullet, tuna, and sturgeon were favorite foods for the rich.

Most poor people added only a little salted fish to their soups and stews, unless their families went fishing. However, some people who farmed near the sea owned boats and fished as well as farmed.

> "In October gales come from all directions. Then keep your ships no longer on the wine-bright sea, but stay and work the land. Protect your ship with close-packed stones to shield it from the mighty winds. Stow all your gear and tackle in the house. Wait till the sailing season comes . . . in springtime.
>
> When a man can first see leaves upon the very tops of fig trees, tiny as the prints the crow makes with her foot, then the sea is passable. . .
>
> Late August is the time to sail, when the heat of summertime is over. Then your ship will not be shattered nor your sailors lost at sea, unless the shaker of the earth, Poseidon, or Zeus wishes to destroy it. At this time the winds are steady and the sea is untroublesome."
>
> from *Works and Days*, by Hesiod

△ The ancient Greeks believed that when Poseidon was angry, he beat the seas with his trident (3-pronged spear) and there were terrible storms.

◁ This temple to Poseidon at Sounion in Attica was built around 440 B.C. The site was once surrounded by strong walls. From Sounion, the Athenians defended their ports on the nearby island of Euboea.

Food in towns and cities

△ The site of the acropolis at Corinth is called Acrocorinth. It is in such a good position that it was used to defend the surrounding area by various peoples and armies until the end of the 18th century A.D.

Water for the towns was often brought in from springs outside it, through clay channels, or **aqueducts**.

"The Athenians brought in from the country their wives and children and all their household goods . . . They sent their sheep and cattle to the islands off the coast."

from *History of the Peloponnesian War*, by Thucydides. The work was begun in 431 B.C.

Few towns and cities in ancient Greece had more than 20,000 people living in them. Sparta was "more like a group of villages" according to Thucydides, the ancient Greek historian, writing in the 5th century BC. However, about 90,000 people lived in Corinth, and 300,000 people lived in the city of Athens at this time.

Cities such as Athens and Corinth grew around an acropolis. This was a site that could be defended and where people from the surrounding countryside found shelter in times of war.

At first, many of the people who lived in the cities also farmed land outside it. Then, as the city-states grew more powerful, the cities themselves became more important as centers for trade and government. More skilled people, such as craftworkers, came to live in the towns and cities.

These workers had no farmland of their own. They had to buy food at the markets. Food was brought in by the farmers or imported from other countries by **merchants** and traders.

▽ Athena was the daughter of Zeus and his first wife, Metis. Athena, the goddess of wisdom, protected the city of Athens, as well as the heroes and craftworkers.

▷ A stone carving of a young girl holding a goose.

▽ This storage jar is called a pelike. It was used to store food supplies or wine. The painting on it shows a woman washing her hair.

"A wife should look after the household so that supplies which are meant to last a year are not used up in a month. . . . Clothes should be made for all who need them; dried foods should be kept in good condition. . . . If slaves are ill then she should look after them."

from *Economics*, by Xenophon, written in the 4th century B.C.

Most households in the towns and cities kept hens, so that they had a supply of fresh eggs to eat. Rich people enjoyed eating peacock or goose eggs instead of hens' eggs. They kept stores of foods such as grain and wine in their houses.

Work in the towns and cities started just before dawn, as it did in the countryside. Women tended the fire, then started weaving cloth or grinding seeds to make flour for bread. Men usually went out of the households to work.

Few people ate more than a snack for breakfast or lunch – a handful of olives or a piece of fruit, some bread and cheese. The main meal was eaten at sunset. For most townspeople this meal was as simple as the food eaten in the countryside.

In Athens, small dishes of food were served after the main course at dinner parties or symposia. Then the music, talking, and drinking began and often lasted through the night.

"It was almost light and the cocks were crowing. . . . Aristophanes and Socrates were still talking and drinking – passing a large bowl around counterclockwise."

from *Symposium*, by Plato, written in the 4th century B.C.

"The cook sets out a large tray on which there are five small plates of food. One of these holds garlic, another a pair of sea urchins, another bread soaked in sweet white wine, another ten cockles, the last a small piece of sturgeon."

from *The Gastronomers*, by Athenaeus

△ Bowls that were used for mixing wine and water were called kraters. They had wide mouths and broad bodies. This bowl was made around the 14th century B.C. The painting on it shows a Mycenaean horseman with a chariot.

The ancient Greeks' idea of the best type of food is described by Telecleides, as part of a wonderful dream, in *The Amphictyons*.

"Every stream ran with wine. Barley pastes fought with wheat loaves to be the first to be eaten. . . . Fish would come to the house and bake themselves, then serve themselves up at the table. A river of soup, swirling along with hot pieces of meat, would flow by the couches; spicy sauces for the meat were close at hand, ready to be poured. . . . There would be dishes of honey cakes, sprinkled with spices, and roast thrushes served with milk cakes flew down a man's throat."

quoted by Athenaeus in *The Gastronomers*

In the 4th century B.C. an Athenian baker called Thearion invented molds for baking bread. The playwright Antiphanes said the "baking pans of various shapes" were used to bake "white-bodied loaves." These were probably made from wheat.

◁ These clay figures show bakers making bread. The loaves are probably made of wheat and have been baked in molds, as they are all roughly the same shape and size.

▷ This man is holding a wine cup called a kantharos.

Unlike many other city-states, Sparta did not build up trade with other places. People continued to exchange, or **barter**, for the goods they needed to buy in the towns. In other city-states, people used money to buy and sell things.

Sparta did not need to import food. The Spartans owned farms that the helots worked for them. A share of the food they produced was brought to the public dining halls, where all Spartan men ate. They were forbidden to work the land themselves or to trade in goods. Spartan men were trained and lived as foot soldiers, or hoplites. Spartan women were trained like the men, to be physically fit, brave, and obedient.

Spartan food was said to be the worst in ancient Greece! One visitor to Sparta, seeing the food being eaten in the public dining hall, said, "Now I understand why Spartans do not fear death." Another visitor, faced with the famous "black broth," said he would jump in the river rather than eat it.

▽ This stone carving was made around 500 BC. It has been named the "Running Hoplite."

Each city-state had its own weights and measures.

Most city-states also made their own silver coins. As Athens grew more powerful than other city-states, Athenian weights, measures, and coins were used everywhere—except in Sparta.

Food for travelers

◁ The painting on this cup, made in the 6th century B.C., shows storage jars full of grain being transported by mules.

Many people in ancient Greece made daily journeys, traveling short distances over land and sea. Farmers took produce to market; fishermen brought their catch into port. The travelers took a snack with them when they left early in the morning and arrived home in time for dinner at sunset. Even rich landowners who rode out to their farms from the city returned in time for a bath and then dinner, according to the writer Xenophon.

Some people traveled to visit holy places, such as Delphi and Olympia, to give offerings to the gods. Xenophon had a temple built to the goddess Artemis at Delphi. He left money to ensure that people were offered bread, wine, cakes, and a share of the game they were allowed to hunt on his land, during the festival to the goddess.

Athletes came from all over Greece to take part in the Olympic Games in honor of Zeus.

▽ The wall painting, shows men at a symposium, which comes from a tomb in southern Italy. The ancient Greeks took their way of life to many parts of Europe.

The ancient Greeks knew that to stay healthy as well as fit, they needed to eat the right foods.

"As far as food and drink are concerned, it is better to know what kinds are wholesome and choose those that are good for the stomach rather than those that taste good."

from "Advice on Keeping Well," in *Moralia*, by Plutarch, written in the 1st century A.D.

▷ This painting shows men weighing out goods on a large balance scale. It was painted on an amphora, made in Attica, which was found in Sicily.

Sailors in merchant ships made long journeys across the Mediterranean Sea. The ships carried goods such as pottery, wine, and olive oil from Greece. They brought back many important cargoes to Greece, such as grain and slaves.

Sailors took stew pots, *kakavin*, with them, so that they could cook fish soups and vegetable stews for their evening meals.

They stayed at Olympia for several weeks, training for the Games. Food and shelter was provided for them.

Poorer people also offered hospitality to travelers. In Euripides' play *Electra*, written in the 5th century B.C., a farmer invites travelers in, saying, "My house is poor, but you are welcome to what I have." Then an old slave fetches a lamb, some cheese, a little wine, and wreaths of flowers for his guests.

Some of the ancient Greeks traveled far from home. People who went to settle in Italy, France, and Egypt traveled by sea. The ships stayed close to the coasts whenever possible.

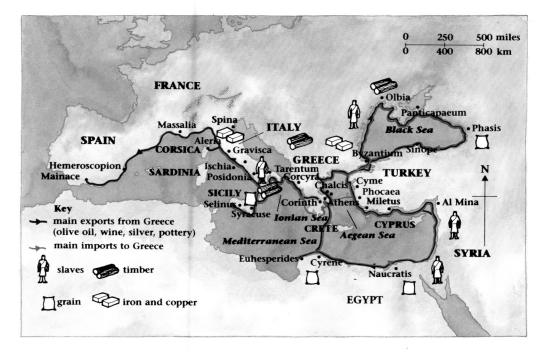

◁ This map shows the main sea routes taken by the ancient Greeks. It also shows the goods they carried and the Greek settlements they visited.

◁ A team of men rowing a trireme, an ancient Greek warship

Soldiers and sailors going to war carried some food, their **rations**, with them, usually barley-paste cakes and water.

When the city-states were at war with each other, they tried to end the fighting as quickly as possible. Many of the soldiers were also farmers. They needed to get back to their land

◁ The ancient Greeks believed that the gods and goddesses enjoyed feasts as much as they did. Here, Persephone is dining with Pluto, the god of the underworld.

to look after their animals and crops.

The armies did not have enough food supplies for a long war. The soldiers' rations would not last for more than a few days. Invading armies would cut down and spoil the crops, to make sure that their enemies were weakened. There was often a food shortage or famine after a war.

Homer describes an outdoor feast that was held for Odysseus on his travels. This feast was probably similar to those eaten by Greek leaders and their warriors at that time.

However, most people in ancient Greece did not eat as well as this, whether they were on their travels or at home. Homer's works were well-known by the ancient Greeks. His descriptions of great meat-eating feasts became part of the stories and **legends** of a wonderful life in the past.

"He put down a large bench in the firelight and laid sheep, a fat goat, and a great joint of hog on it. Achilles carved them up, putting the pieces on spits. Meanwhile Patroclus made the fire blaze up. When it burned down again, he scattered the embers and laid the spits above them, resting them on logs, after he had sprinkled the meat with salt. When he had roasted it and heaped it up on platters, Patroclus fetched some bread and set it out on the table in baskets and Achilles divided the meat into portions."

from Homer's *Odyssey*

▷ Some archaeologists think that many of Homer's stories are based on fact.
This gold drinking cup was made in the 15th century B.C., long before Homer's *Odyssey* was composed. It shows a hunter in the forest, tying up a wild bull.

Meals and recipes

Many of the dishes served in Greece today are the same as those enjoyed by the ancient Greeks. Olive oil, garlic, yogurt, honey, and herbs are still widely used in the preparation and cooking of Greek food. People still grill fresh fish and cook meat and vegetables on skewers over an open charcoal fire.

However, the ways in which we preserve foods today, by canning and freezing, had not been invented in the time of the ancient Greeks. The taste of foods that have been preserved by drying, salting, and pickling is quite different from the taste of canned or frozen foods.

Citrus fruits, such as oranges and lemons, were not grown in ancient Greece, and foods such as potatoes and tomatoes from the Americas were unknown. Honey was used as a sweetener, rather than sugar.

Most people ate food that was produced locally. There were no planes, trucks, or trains to transport food quickly around the world. The choice of fresh fruit, vegetables, and herbs depended on what was grown locally in each season.

In winter there was less fresh food. People ate more preserved foods – dried fruit and vegetables such as figs, raisins, and beans, and pickled, smoked, or salted fish.

> **WARNING:** Sharp knives and boiling liquids are dangerous. Hot ovens and pans can burn you. *Always ask an adult to help you* when you are preparing or cooking food in the kitchen.

Tzatziki
(Yogurt and garlic dip)

You can serve this dish with sticks of fresh raw celery and carrots, a bowl of green or black olives, and fresh pita bread.

Ingredients

2 cloves garlic

1/2 tsp salt

1 tsp black pepper

2 T olive oil

1 T white wine vinegar

2 1/2 cups thick creamy yogurt

1. Peel the skin off the cloves of garlic. Crush the cloves in a garlic press *or* carefully chop them very fine with a sharp knife. Be sure to keep your fingers away from the knife blade.
2. Put the garlic, salt, and pepper into a small mixing bowl.
3. Measure out the olive oil and vinegar and mix them thoroughly with the garlic using a wooden spoon.
4. Measure out the yogurt and put it into a serving bowl. Then add the garlic mixture and stir it into the yogurt until it blends well.
5. Chill the *tzatziki* in the refrigerator for about two hours and then serve.

Equipment

garlic press *or* sharp knife and chopping board

measuring spoons

small mixing bowl

measuring cup

wooden spoon

serving bowl

Ask an adult to help you when you start to cook.

Savoro

(Pickled fish)

Ingredients

1 1/4 lb fresh fillets of sardines, herring, *or* mackerel

1 medium-sized onion

3 celery stalks

3 cloves garlic

1/3 cup olive oil

1/2 tsp dried thyme

1/4 tsp dried rosemary

1 bay leaf

1/2 cup white wine vinegar

1/2 tsp salt

1 tsp black pepper

1 T finely chopped fresh parsley

1. Put the fish fillets in a colander and wash them thoroughly in cold running water. Then leave them in the colander to dry.
2. Peel the onion and chop it into small pieces with a sharp knife. Be sure to keep your fingers away from the knife blade.
3. Wash the celery stalks and then carefully chop them into small pieces with a sharp knife.
4. Peel the skin off the cloves of garlic and carefully chop them very fine with a sharp knife.
5. Measure out 3 T of the olive oil into the skillet. Then fry the onion gently in the olive oil until it starts to change color.
6. Add the celery and garlic to the onion and stir the mixture with a wooden spoon.
7. Measure out the thyme and rosemary and add these and the bay leaf to the vegetables in the skillet.
8. Remove the skillet from the heat. Then measure out the vinegar. Pour half of it into the skillet and add the salt and pepper.
9. Stir the mixture well and put the skillet back on the heat. Cook the mixture gently for 10 minutes. Then take the skillet off the heat.

Equipment

colander

sharp knife

chopping board

measuring cup

measuring spoons

large skillet

wooden spoon

large shallow serving dish

Ask an adult to help you when you start to cook.

Sharp knives, hot liquids, and hot pans are dangerous.

10. Add the fish to the mixture in the skillet and stir it well.
11. Put the skillet back on the heat and cook the fish for about 5-8 minutes if you are using sardines, 8-12 minutes if you are using herring, and 15 minutes if you are using mackerel. Then spoon the mixture into the serving dish. Remove the bay leaf.
12. Carefully chop the parsley very fine. Be sure to keep your fingers away from the blade of the knife.
13. Sprinkle the parsley over the mixture in the serving dish. Then add the rest of the vinegar.
14. Pour the rest of the olive oil over the mixture so that the oil covers the surface completely.
15. When the mixture has cooled, put the dish into the refrigerator for at least 24 hours before serving.

Souvlakia
(Meat on skewers)

Ingredients
4 cloves garlic
1½ lb thick cubes of pork *or* lamb
1 cup white grape juice
2 T olive oil
1 tsp dried oregano
1 tsp black pepper
½ tsp salt

Ask an adult to help you when you start to cook.

1. Peel the skin off the cloves of garlic. Crush the cloves in a garlic press *or* carefully chop them very fine with a sharp knife. Be sure to keep your fingers away from the knife blade.
2. Put the garlic in a large mixing bowl. Then measure out all the other ingredients and add them to the garlic.
3. Mix everything together thoroughly with a wooden spoon so that the meat is well covered with all the other ingredients.
4. Put the bowl in the refrigerator for at least four hours or overnight.
5. Remove the meat cubes from the mixture and throw the liquid away.
6. Put the meat cubes on skewers.
7. Ask an adult to cook the skewered cubes on a barbecue *or* under a broiler.

Equipment
garlic press *or* sharp knife and chopping board
large mixing bowl
measuring cup
measuring spoons
wooden spoon
8 skewers
barbecue *or* broiler

Sharp knives are dangerous.

Ingredients

2 lb spinach, *or*
   1 lb beet tops

water

1 T olive oil

2 tsp white wine
   vinegar

salt

**Ask an adult to
help you when
you start to cook.**

Horta
(Green leafy vegetables)

The Greeks make this dish from the leaves of any
green vegetable in season, including those
growing wild. *Horta* is sometimes eaten on its
own – it is said to help settle the stomach—or to
accompany meatballs or fried fish.

1. Carefully trim the leaves and cut out the thick
   stems from the vegetables with a sharp knife.
   Be sure to keep your fingers away from the
   knife blade.
2. Wash the vegetables very carefully under cold
   running water and put them in the colander
   to drain.
3. If you are using spinach, place it in a large
   saucepan with very little water. If you are
   using beet tops, place them in a large
   saucepan with about $1/2$ cup water.
4. Bring the water to a boil. Cover the saucepan
   with a lid and reduce the heat.
5. Simmer the spinach for about 3-4 minutes
   or the beet tops for about 5-6 minutes, until
   the vegetables are tender.
6. Ask an adult to use the colander to drain the
   vegetables and place them in the serving dish.
7. Measure out the oil and vinegar and mix them
   into the vegetables with a wooden spoon.
   Season with salt to taste.
8. This dish can be served hot or cold.

Equipment

sharp knife

chopping board

colander

large saucepan

measuring spoons

serving dish

wooden spoon

Sharp knives, hot
liquids, and hot
pans are dangerous.

Ingredients

$1/4$ cup chopped
   walnuts *or*
   almonds

$1/4$ cup clear honey

$2^1/2$ cups thick
   creamy yogurt

Yogurt with honey and nuts

Both walnut and almond trees grew in ancient
Greece, but they probably came from what is now
Turkey. The Persians called walnuts Greek nuts
while the Romans called almonds Greek nuts.

1. Measure out all the ingredients and put them
   in the mixing bowl.
2. Stir the mixture well with a wooden spoon
   and leave it for five minutes.
3. Spoon the mixture into the serving bowls and
   serve immediately, or leave in the refrigerator
   to keep cool.

Equipment

measuring cup

mixing bowl

wooden spoon

serving bowls

Glossary

altar: A flat-topped block or table on which offerings are placed for gods and goddesses.

amphora: A tall, narrow jar made of pottery, used to store liquids such as wine or olive
(pl. amphorae) oil.

aqueduct: A bridge or channel built to carry water. The ancient Greeks used pipes made of clay, and they carved channels from stone.

archaeologist: Someone who studies the past by digging up or examining ancient ruins and remains.

artifact: An object that people make and use.

banquet: A grand feast or public dinner.

bartering: A form of buying and selling by exchanging goods instead of using money. The Athenians were the first to use coins instead of bartering goods. The Spartans used iron bars rather than coins when they could not barter for the goods they needed.

cauldron: A large pot, usually made of iron, for boiling water and cooking over an open fire.

charcoal: Small pieces of burnt wood, used for fuel.

city-state: A small state or area of land. Its center is a single city, which governs it.

cultivate: To grow plants or to prepare and use soil for planting crops.

democracy: A word, originally from Greek, describing the way in which a state or country is ruled. In a democracy, the leaders are chosen freely by the people.

drought: An unusually long period without rain or snow.

elect: To vote for one person from a group of people. The winners become the leaders or other important officials.

erode: To wear away the surface of something and destroy it.

excavate: To dig up buried objects or remains from the past, such as buildings, in a scientific manner. Archaeologists excavate sites to find out more about how people lived in earlier times.

export: To send or take goods from one country to sell in another.

famine: A time when there is not enough food, so people starve.

forage: To wander freely, looking for food.

game: Animals, birds, and fish that are hunted for food or for sport.

ham: Meat, from the leg of a pig, that has been salted and dried to keep it from spoiling.

herb: A plant used either in cooking (to add flavor to food) or as a medicine.

import: To bring goods from one country to sell in another.

irrigate: To bring water to crops.

legend: An old story that many people believe, even though it may not be quite true.

merchants: People who buy and sell goods, often from different countries. Merchants in ancient Greece sometimes owned the transportation—ships, horses, carts, or camels—they organized to take goods from one place to another.

preserve: To treat food or drink so that it can be kept for a long time without spoiling. The main ways of preserving food in ancient Greece were salting, drying, pickling, and smoking. Salt, pepper, vinegar, and oil were used in preserving food. Frozen and canned foods were unknown at this time.

quern: A stone hand mill, used for grinding grain into flour.

rations: Limited amounts of food, such as those issued to soldiers or sailors.

skewer: A metal or wooden spike, used to hold meat together while it is being cooked.

spit: A long, thin metal bar, often pointed, on which food is placed to be cooked.

staple: The most important or main food, crop, or goods produced in a particular area.

subsistence: The way people support themselves to stay alive. In subsistence farming, almost all the produce is used by the farmer's household. There is little or nothing left over to give or sell to others.

surplus: Something left over, after all that is needed has been used.

terrace: A flat piece of ground that is cut like a large step into the side of a hill.

trivet: A three-legged stand for a pot, usually made of iron.

Further reading

Artman, John. *Ancient Greece*. Good Apple, 1991.

Burrell, Roy. *The Greeks*. Rebuilding the Past series. Oxford University Press, 1990.

Cohen, Daniel. *Ancient Greece*. Doubleday, 1990.

Connolly, Peter. *The Legend of Odysseus*. Oxford University Press, 1991.

Edmondson, Elizabeth. *The Trojan War*. Great Battles and Sieges series. New Discovery Books, 1992.

Lerner Geography Staff. *Greece in Pictures*. Visual Geography series. Lerner Publications, 1991.

Pearson, Anne. *Ancient Greece*. Eyewitness Books. Knopf, 1992.

Sauvain, Philip. *Over 2000 Years Ago in Ancient Greece*. History Detective series. New Discovery Books, 1992.

Spyropulos, Diana. *Greece: A Spirited Independence*. Discover Our Heritage series. Dillon Press, 1990.

Steele, Philip. *Thermopylae*. Great Battles and Sieges series. New Discovery Books, 1993.

Tyler, Deborah. *The Greeks and Troy*. Hidden Worlds series. Dillon Press, 1993.

Williams, A. Susan. *The Greeks*. Look into the Past series. Thomson Learning, 1993.

Index